VORTEX OF INDIAN FEVERS

VORTEX
OF
INDIAN
FEVERS

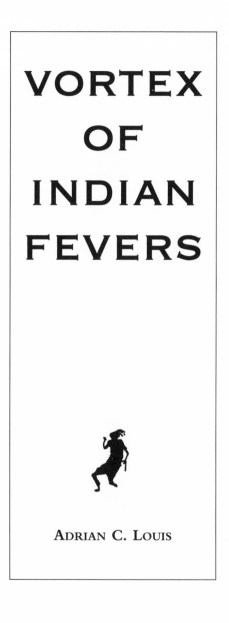

ADRIAN C. LOUIS

TRIQUARTERLY BOOKS
NORTHWESTERN UNIVERSITY PRESS

TriQuarterly Books
Northwestern University Press
Evanston, Illinois 60208-4210

Copyright © 1995 by Adrian C. Louis
Printed in the United States of America
All rights reserved

Library of Congress Cataloging-in-Publication Data

Louis, Adrian C.
    Vortex of Indian fevers / Adrian C. Louis.
        p.   cm.
    ISBN 0-8101-5017-4 (alk. paper). —
    ISBN 0-8101-5042-5 (pbk. : alk.
    paper)
    1. Indians of North America—Poetry. I. Title.
    PS3562.082V67   1995
    811'.54—dc20   94-45837
                                          CIP

The paper used in this publication meets the minimum
requirements of the American National Standard for
Information Sciences—Permanence of Paper for Printed
Library Materials, ANSI 39.48-1984.

This book of poems
is for Colleen
and in memory
of Robert Gay (1946–93)

There's still the hardship, there's still the pain.
There's still the hardship, there's still the strife.
Its bitterness shines like a whetted knife.
There's still the hypocrisy, and still the hate.
Was that in the treaties, was that our fate?
We're all unhappy pawns in the government's
    game. And it's always the native
who gets the blame.

—Willie Dunn

CONTENTS

III

Acknowledgments

Grateful acknowledgment is made to the editors of the following publications in which some of these poems first appeared:

The Kenyon Review, Ploughshares, TriQuarterly, The Southern Review, North Dakota Quarterly, New Letters, Caliban, Exquisite Corpse, Akwe:kon, Context South, Kumquat Meringue, Atom Mind, Blue Mesa Review, Long Shot, Chiron Review, Lactuca, Prairie Winds, Owen Wister Review, Whiskey Island Magazine, and *Chicago Review.*

Several of these poems, some in earlier versions, also appeared in *Sweets for the Dancing Bears* and *Muted War Drums,* chapbooks from Blue Cloud Abbey Press. Others first saw light in an anthology from Poetry Harbor Press entitled *Days of Obsidian, Days of Grace.*

I

GNAWING OLD BONES

STATUE OF LIBERTY

Wondrous woman!
Eurydice will not do to compare you to.
Your myth isn't current or primal.
An androgynous scorpion with mothering
claws and stinger behind, you wrench
the victims from the dry loins of earth
and inject their dazzled brains
with the harsh flame of hope.
Cold, worn gears whine inside
your bronzed vulva and dark bodies
are dropped to the tired sea.
Like legions of smiling buoys,
they bob toward that cruel illusion
we choose to call freedom.
But beyond their gleeful yammer,
I can hear faint clicking sounds
filling the awkward gaps
in their prayers of thanks.

When I listen closely I don't hear
the midnight ride of Paul Revere
but ghosts of dead tribes
bonesinging under concrete.

Human Brain Song

Scanning a dunning letter
as I left the Pine Ridge post office,
I stumbled upon Verdell's cousin Franklin.
He was passed out cold on the earth
and I blindly walked onto him.
In a furious blur, he came to kicking
and swinging in a bottle-fight stupor
and let out a shattering girlish squeal.
Surprised adrenalin surging, I shrieked
even louder, *eeeeyiiiiii!!*
like I'd stepped on a timber rattler
and Franklin lurched to his feet
in a boxer's stance.

Franklin, that crazy old drunk.
Was he assuming a Sioux position,
snoring upon green, shattered glass?
Beneath the sun of doom with his face
frying upon the nickel, who was crying
as flies counted coup and danced
on his dying eyes?
It was not me. I could not cry,
but I almost did when he borrowed
the strength to stand up and fight
from the buzzed-up spirits in his brain.
I felt like smashing him, but I walked on.
I walked on, but I almost went back

to shake old Franklin and say
I was sorry in fists so soft
they'd pass
for caresses.

VERDELL'S VIEW OF CRAZY HORSE

Inside the post office a poster
displays new stamps: romantic Indian war
bonnets in hues never seen by our ancestors.

Outside, bruised and bumbling
unsika winos trod by with Hefty bags
full of flattened beer cans.

On dilapidated Main Street
moans of Christmas carols curiously float
from Big Bat's Conoco Station and Mini-Mart.

In a frozen fissure on the uplifted pavement
an empty crack vial sleeps.
Grandfather! Can this plastic clue

to unhappiness be anything else but our own fault?
Despite the fact that the outside world
now haunts this nation with white man dreams,

it's really like my friend Verdell always says:
"When Tasunke Witko was murdered
that day at Fort Robinson
the last living free Indian died."

HALF-BREED'S SONG

for Janet Campbell Hale

Late March. The High Plains.
The idyllic intrudes briefly.
The playful Dakota sun burnishes
the hoar frost on cedars
and winter's nightmares are melting.
Kids are tightrope walking
the snow-packed streets to school.
A sudden warm wind gently shakes
the neighbor lady's clothesline
flock of blue, white, and pink panties.
I pull out the snarls and braid
my burden of waist-length hair.
When I first left home
more than a quarter of a century ago,
I had a flat-top with wings.
I took a job in a Reno casino
making change for fools at the slots.
My sister has a photo of me from those days.
What a strange, muscular clown I was.
Striped, button-down shirt, Hush Puppies
and pressed corduroy slacks
and that goofy flat-top with wings.

No men wore braids back then
and I was ashamed of my Indian blood.
Grandfather . . . no shit, sometimes
I still am.

How Verdell and Dr. Zhivago
Disassembled the Soviet Union

"You are the blessing in a stride towards perdition when living sickens more than sickness itself."—Boris Pasternak

Last year, before cruising to the warehouse
near the old Moccasin Factory,
Verdell and I stopped at the bootlegger
for a quick belt to cinch
his stomach full of fears.
He said the pint of rotgut whiskey
tasted worse than gangrene
but it did the job and choked silent
the raging world around him.
We meandered through tons
of remaindered and donated tomes,
a tax-deductible donation
to destitute savages, these boxed words
were stacked from concrete floor
to rusted sheet-metal roof.
Buzzed-up and warmed by his whiskey,
Verdell came upon four cartons
of Pasternak's *Doctor Zhivago*
and became transfixed by the flaming
scarlet fake leather covering.

But I saw dead ikons of the past
in cardboard and glory on the grandest scale.
Deep in Holy Mother Russia
marching through the bitter snow

I saw peasant armies mouthing
death songs while
not knowing where
their souls would go.

We lugged those four cartons of *Zhivago*
bound in leatherette
to his puke-stained Plymouth.
That spring, without an ounce of shame
and some pride, Verdell related how
he had liked the Russian story,
but he said he ran out of firewood
during the last blizzard of March
and his hungry woodstove
vaporized Yurii Andreievich,
sweet Lara, and those eerie blue wolves
howling at snowbound Varykino.
Again and again, Verdell burned the books
until the cast iron glowed a deep, dark red
and the way he figured it, the heat
from his woodstove melted the glue
of the Soviet Union that spring.

LA CARGA

April 24, 1982, my thirty-fifth birthday
and I'm naked with Evaline Perez inside
the cancerous burrito of gray L.A. springtime.
I open the window and ever-moving traffic
mutes Mexican words I can't make out.
Across Pico some twelve-year-old
diez y ocho peewees are strutting,
flashing gangster hand signals and one child
lifts his shirt to show his homeboys
blue steel which is hidden.
I look under my pillow and stroke
my own 9-mm. shooting iron.
This gray-aired hell is America
and every step in my life
had led me here and it damn sure
smells like the end of my road.
This ain't no nursery rhyme, Eva says
and smack dab in the middle of her vein,
a cow jumps up from the spoon.
It's a big, slobbering milk-tit cow
and it kisses her down
into sweet, snoring sleep.

POSTSCRIPT: DEVILS TOWER

for Scott Momaday

There is nothing to do but pray.
Grandfather, I am humbled.
Grandfather, I am small.
I am little with less character
than the turds of a rabbit.
I am insignificant. This massive lodge
of sky-pillaging stone could easily rape the moon.
Grandfather, forgive all my sins.

I trudge up a small rise and squat in a burgeoning
stand of young aspen. At the base of the tower
four rock climbers prepare their ascent unaware
that from the top their God is invisible
and can only be seen from the base.
The tower rises, the tower rises.
The Empire State Building is nothing.
Hoover Dam is tons of cement.
All man-made glory is a child's toy.

Grandfather, forgive me.
Make me strong.
Let me taste our red nations before the white man.
Let me speak in the spirit,
in the voice of the warrior.

Grandfather, I am the buffalo ghost.
Grandfather, I am the bear clawing rock
and I'm knocking on the door
to your house.

AKICITA OLOWAN

for Bob, brother, friend, scholar, gone.

Not far from that bar in Interior,
I stopped the car on the lonely highway
and got out to say a prayer.
There, where brutal icewinds drank
the last of your brown warrior warmth,
one of autumn's golden cottonwood
leaves poked up from the melting snow.
The tattered, tired leaf shimmered
and repelled bright sunlight kisses
too shy to pierce the frigid depths.
For a second, I forced myself to think
of how cottonwood trees were always
placed in the center of the sundance grounds
and then I could no longer prevent
the bitter, cold vision of how it must have been
when the ice spirits came to fight you.
Kola, they said you'd grown whiskey
muscles when your car went off the road
into the sharp-ice and below zero snow.
That you must have lowered your head
and strolled off into the swirling air,
seeing the distant lights of Kadoka,
maybe thinking them to be your home Wanblee,
maybe thinking you were still young
and invincible, but ending up twisted and frozen
like that picture of Chief Bigfoot.

Not far from that bar in Interior,
I stopped the car on the lonely highway
and got out to say a prayer.
Life still had me hog tied and thrashing.
Halfway past my fortieth year
and flat-ass broke with ever increasing
body malfunctions, I was still assessing
and assigning blame for the creation
of mankind and lately had started
to say "The Lord's Prayer" backwards
before I augered my head into pillows.

Kola, that was a hard place to be
and what I said was not much of a prayer.
Let's call it *akicita olowan.*
A warrior song for you, my brother.

Rhetorical Judea

Most of my life I courted simplicity
and tried to leash any wind-breaking plagues
of rhetoric that swirled in my brain.
I prayed for rational segues from word
to deed, pain to relief, and madness to sanity
with little success so sometimes words
surged like mad lemmings to my tongue
and I spoke from a lopsided ether.

Most of my life had been led without Jesus.
Young, I built a tower around him from bricks
of doubt cemented with white lies
but he busted out and is sneaking around.
We all change. The great cliché I used to run to
was "misspent youth." Quaint, but yes,
at nineteen I became an alley cat,
snarling and spitting on cheap wine,
dining in rescue mission soup lines,
and humping anything on two legs.
No golden coin of the realm
was used in my rutting.
My one-eyed divining rod literally
led me by the hand for two decades.
Now, I'm scared to death of dying,
and I feel compelled to confess to the world!
I'm addicted to television and the IRS
is on my ass, but I shun those

who don't shun excess.
My latest God's eye is this:
I've abandoned those
who seek wild abandon.

This year I have been praying to stop
my rhetoric from defiling wisdom and maybe
that's the reason why I won't get drunk
and chase women with Verdell
who can't get past thinking the white man
tossed us down this sewer and we can't get out.
I've tried to tell him that we've become addicted
to eating shit, that we like the rank taste and tune.
I've tried to tell him many things
but his full-blood ass just won't listen
and the Great Spirit . . . well, the Great Spirit
needs his ears dewaxed
and Jesus, Jesus Christ of rhetorical Judea,
now paging Jesus, now paging Jesus!

BONESINGING THOSE RED BLUES

I

Sometimes you grow tired of gnawing
old bones, those remnants
of a life lived in the ecstasy of rage
and sometimes you become a rabid
cur, angered and ravenous for bones
buried in forgotten locations
of your brain-yard.

II

From sleep hills of horror
the thunderbird screamed
at your graveyard of dreams:
A spirit boy sobbed
for his sword-hacked mother
in a wail more nerve-wracking
than the Great Spirit's deathsong.
From Nevada to Dakota and back again,
lesser deities danced in violent aerial anger.
Oh, your dream. Your terrible dream.
Spirits of rock, tree and water
silently prayed for your buckskin race
whose frozen mud eyes
were bled of their vision
of desperate dancing.

Now awake, exactly one hundred years
later beneath the lone, stone
pillar at Wounded Knee
blood flows from your ears.
Here, in this air, are the whispers
of hundreds of old men and women,
young boys and warriors
murdered under a white flag of truce.

III

There is so much that you have forgotten.
America has always been blind to the past,
and because of this, it has no soul.
Last year when a Japanese company
wanted to buy the concession business
at Yellowstone Park, the yip-yap patriots
whined remembered hints of Iwo Jima,
Guadalcanal and Corregidor.
But nobody asked the trees their opinion.
Nobody asked the bears to shit their feelings.
You're no bear or tree, but you know that
recently, a flickering red paper sun
has come to you in dreams.
It rises in glory between calm blue seas
and playful white clouds and the ghost
choruses of Hiroshima and Nagasaki whisper
every painful, shameful word of explanation
our government has ever invented.

You do not claim moral superiority
but some mornings when you awake
you smell barbecued children
and see molten puddles
of pregnant women
and you wonder where
all the bombs are sleeping now.

IV

Summer came and you were back in Nevada
after six years of your latest lam.
The welcoming sun anointed your head
with holy, delirious sweat.
The dry Great Basin welcomed you home.
A trumpet-blast wind blew
singing sand past your exiled ears.
You felt as free as free could be
and jumped up and ran with dust devils,
singing and crying with pure Paiute joy.
You hyperventilated, purging your lungs
of all purloined blues.
You whirled like a stepped-on diamondback
and beheld the miracle-mirage
of no telephone poles as far as you could see.
The great cancer of technology was in remission.
You screamed *aiiiiieeeee* and jackrabbits dashed
into the sacred four directions.
The court jester coyote smiled and hooted
and whispered that America
dropped A-bombs here.

You still remember the palsied earth, but you
remember one stronger earth pain:
In Nevada, until 1953, Indians were not allowed
out into white towns after dark.
Upon that soil where they'd danced
for thousands of years, somehow, your people
fell through the cracks in the Liberty Bell.
In Nevada, until 1953, Indians were not allowed
out into white towns after dark.
O Nevada, your sweet native land.
Your Nevada, a deep cesspool of greed.
A welcomer of whorehouses, strip mines,
casinos and hydrogen bombs.
All upon this soil where your ancestors are buried.
All upon this land where Wovoka tied your Paiute
people to the mass grave at Wounded Knee.
Now you understand with your erotic heart,
those stories of Japanese soldiers
still marching to the Emperor's beat
on small islands a decade past V-J Day.
You know that when they were discovered,
some went joyously berserk,
weapons raised into the finality of defeat.
Some sat with their bowls of rice
and ignored the new ghosts
who had not been invited to dinner.
Others sat calmly collected
and with great relief,
they disemboweled themselves.

END PRAYER FOR MOGIE

"I'm cutting back on my drinking
but I feel like the devil's breathing
down my drawers," Mogie said
and drank the spider inside
the green-glassed pint.

That week my old friend
started to carry around a small
brown bottle of nitroglycerin
pills per doctor's orders
"on his person" just in case
his heart decided to sing pain.

Sure, he was weary, but damn it,
he was not even close to being ready
to check out of this cheap motel.
He still had love to give.
Mogie still had *olowan* to sing.
He had phantom, unplanned steps to add
to his Indian cheap wine ballet.
When he took sick, I said King's X
a thousand times for him, but the Sky God
was frantic with spring cleaning.
Took out his cosmic Hoover.
Sucked old Mogie's soul away.

II

VORTEX OF INDIAN FEVERS

LOOKING FOR JUDAS

Weathered gray, the wooden walls
of the old barn soak in the bright
sparkling blood of the five-point mule
deer I hang there in the moonlight.
Gutted, skinned, and shimmering in eternal
nakedness, the glint in its eyes could
be stolen from the dry hills of Jerusalem.
They say before the white man
brought us Jesus, we had honor.
They say when we killed the Deer People,
we told them their spirits
would live in our flesh.
We used bows of ash, no spotlights, no rifles,
and their holy blood became ours.
Or something like that.

JUST ANOTHER SUICIDE NOTE
for Patrick Stanhope

Six A.M. on this Indian reservation. I'm on the couch in my shorts watching The Weather Channel and drinking decaf. I let the dogs out and they hop off the porch, pee, then howl to be let in. This blizzard is two months early and it's not just a freak storm. It started the day before Halloween and has been going on for two weeks now. Dumb-ass leaves on my Lombardy poplars have frozen into lime-green popsicles and pull the branches toward the snowy ground. I haven't even winterized my car yet. I let the dogs in and get another cup and hear the old lady upstairs getting ready for work. When she leaves I will take a hot shower and pee and shave in the shower. Then I'll have a shot of whiskey and then go back to bed but not before I put on a rubber and pray for a wet dream in which Jack Kerouac returns from his bloated death and gives me a ghostly handjob and then introduces me to his buddy Elvis who will be dressed like Aunt Jemima and will cook me the yummiest cool daddy-o flapjacks or maybe some grits.

Fever Journal

Dakotah Territory: Mid-September

Bates, Bates, God damn Robert Bates,
last night I dreamed of you and
the time we jumped in that irrigation ditch
down past Campbell ranch and grabbed foot-long
carp with our bare hands and threw
them on the bank and then jumped
on their heads until their
eyeballs popped out into the air
like the slimy green loogies
old men with bad lungs launched.

Bates, I thrashed around all last night like a carp,
sweating with endless chapters
of dick-chilling nightmares
of everything I ever did wrong.
Woke up on the couch at 2 A.M.
and watched PBS about JFK
and the "magic bullet" of Dallas.
Up this morning at 7 to cook coffee.
Fell back asleep waiting for it to brew
and woke by my woman at 10 calling
collect to ask if I wanted her to fix me
homemade chicken soup for dinner.
She said she'd be home from work
early to take care of me.

Bates, I'm so sick I'm peeing in a jar.
My man, when I was hiding from that terminal
Asian jungle disease twenty years ago
I forever lost track of you.
Hiding from my age twenty
days ago I had an affair
and my woman found out
and almost beheaded the old one-eyed
carp who swims around in my pants.
I'm sick. Sicker than I've ever been.
Oh, Bates, you old rat fucker.
At sixteen we sliced our wrists
and became blood brothers.
Made a solemn pact that when we married
we could screw each other's wives.
Bates, I don't know if you're living or dead.
Bates, I don't know if I'm
living or dead.

ANCESTOR PRAYER

for Jimmy Santiago Baca

Cousin, if I shot coke or smack or crank,
my heart would explode or crumple
so I got no choice but to pray.
Ancestor spirits!
What is there I can recall
that will dissolve
this vortex of fever and fear?
Clorox won't do the job.
Ammonia won't shatter the nightmare
and I find no solace in the words
of the effete white poets
on my dusty bookshelves
who claim to be pals with Mr. Death.
Yeah, it's that funky Mr. Death sneaking
around my house in his droopy drawers.
I smell his liquored breath when I whisper
secrets into my cupped hands.
So, ancestor spirits! Hear me now.
Ancestor spirits! Heal me now.
Ancestor spirits! Heal all
us damn fool survivors.

VORTEX OF INDIAN FEVERS
If you got the dinero, I got my Camaro.—Freddy Fender

I

Over a hundred and five degrees for the third
straight day. I placed my face upon the icy grate of our
second-hand fridge next to two senile grapefruits.
Blue and hairy with splotches of mold, they could've
been the scrotum of Tutankhamen. I bought them
the month before, vowing firm flesh more solid than
my sweating nose, flash-frozen to iron near King
Tut's nuts.

Somewhere galaxies of angels were laughing at me.
I was stuck in some Roadrunner cartoon and it
wasn't funny at all. Breaking free, I stamped my feet
and hopped to the sink to warm water my nose and
wished I could go sit and swill in some lonely bar
with the ghosts of my ghosts and taste the cool juice
of fear on their lips but my old lady was driving me
to the hospital when she got back from teaching the
disruptive kids of dysfunctional parents.

II

Sweat-soaked and flaming, I ignored your soothing
as you sped me to the hospital. My crazed concern
was guilt for murdering my black lab last summer
after he bit a little girl. *Do those who kill dogs go to
heaven?* Oh, he was happy, that happy dog. But was
he happy, his happy dog ghost? And what of me,

too coward to shoot him who paid the vet for the needle? I was burning in hell as you drove us toward the hospital. I had endless visions of that child he bit and sent to the stitchers. In the vortex of Indian fevers, I knew I'd be better off had I bit her instead because in the middle of bone-rattling chills, he still whined inside my flaming tongue.

III

When they strapped me down to die, I think I put on a warrior face, sighed and told them that the mere fact of the blade's sharpness was meaningless to me. *Just bury me out on the lone prairie* some macho fool screamed in my skull. And when it was time, I tried to take back my words. *Hey, Mr. Hitler-looking anesthesiologist! Please.* I always sought the road of deep truth and my memory, not rerouted but trafficked so often over the same territory always became the ghost of itself. Okay, so there were times I saw Jehovah through chemical windows so real they allowed fresh air to pierce the concentric circles of my personal hell, but don't leave me wallowing in this dusty butt-plug of a high plains hospital or I'll scream rap lyrics until you unstrap me and let me
moonwalk home.

IV

The patient in the bed beside me said invisible air piranha took turns prodding him toward the gates of Sodom. The three Wise Men, now giftless, wrote angry invoices in the alternate universe of an anteroom or was it the anteroom of an alternate universe? It really didn't matter to him. He was told there would be no holidays from then on.

V

Green-clad cowboys carrying silver knives surrounded my gall bladder and stabbed it to death. I awoke in stitches and fell back to gauze-soft sleep. My hospital bed galloped through morphine dreams of broken arrows scattered in piles on the street corners, on the dirt roads, in the back alleys and the cottonwood valleys of my life.

The broken arrows whispered: *The road you are walking has no beginning, no middle and maybe no end. It's an old Indian curse. Life's true beauty is that it soon ends so always make sure you at least got clean underwear snuggling your precious jewels.*

VI

Through the blur of pain and chemical residue I could see she was Indian, gray-haired and kind. Most of the nurses in that Indian hospital were uniform white but that was all right because I felt so patriotic: I was half-white, half-red and bluer than the blue-veiner standing erect near her hands soaping my balls and ass. She told how she always wanted to be a nurse and when she asked what I wanted to be as a child I shrugged and said I don't know (but don't stop now!). *Old woman, you did understand, now didn't you?*

Back then it was always shit on a shingle or beans or deer meat for supper. Later, after I scoured my underwear in a tin tub and strung them on a rope above a woodstove, I had Indian dreams of pure, white cities. Cities of alabaster. Cities of blond girls. Sweet white nurses in tight white panties. Oh, sweet liquid dreams. My tender foolish dreams. Dear kind gray-haired Indian nurse. I'd tell you the dreams of a half-breed man-child light years ago if you promised, old woman, you'd keep your red hands kneading
my half-red
flesh.

VII

Second day post-op on morphine I dreamed myself to death. My demise took me in a checkered sport coat to a prom where everyone was doing the Mashed Potato or the Frug. And there they were, as biblically promised, all the dear ones I used to love. All the lost friends of childhood had met me on Heaven's shore which looked suspiciously like a high-school gym with awkward harp music and angel food cake! In one crepe-draped corner of the festooned gym were all the forgotten women who curled their noses while they swallowed my angry, young juices. They were carrying *Ginsus*. Sharp, goddamn *Ginsus!* Those television knives that can sever a tin can and then glide through a blood-red tomato. They were whittling a cross for my grave. I whispered as much of the rosary as my scared soul remembered.   My ex–old ladies just smiled and flashed those nasty-sharp

Japanese *Ginsus*.

VIII

Three days after surgery they hooked electrodes to my armpits, chest, ankles and I stared at the ceiling panels, counting the dots and truly glad that I had clean bloomers on. Each acoustic square had eleven hundred forty-seven dots exactly. Yes, I could connect them but the only portrait that surfaced was of that man who was at the Garden of Gethsemane and I knew he'd long ago forsaken me but then I lived so maybe he hadn't. "O Christ, materialize. Straighten my sad ass out," I screamed in

silence.

IX

When I thought I was dying, I did not see a world out of control. I couldn't feel this nation disintegrating. Nor did I smell my body growing old. I had a hunger beyond worry. I had an emptiness that I filled at my leisure with the faces of lost loves. Then I became much sicker. The distant clarion of the carrion eaters did not amaze these ears attuned to tubes. After the operation, after the surgeons tried to corral my slippery gall bladder for eight straight hours, I asked the nurse to turn on the TV. She smiled and clicked it on and I lensed the leeches sucking the blood of this idiot nation and the talons of time clawed my soul open.

In some dark valley of deep medication, I heard Crazy Horse whisper: "Home is where my ancestors lie buried." In the flow of sweet morphine I heard Crazy Horse giggle lowly and say: "Boy, don't you go now and waste your vote on some strange Nazi dwarf."

X

My dogs were barking at the morning sun sliced by venetian blinds. I was delivered from dreams, ghastly dreams of breath's betrayal. My shorts were damp from nightmare sweating. O no-no-no, it was not the night sweats. It was not the night sweats, thank Mary. Mary, Blessed Virgin, I was healing, but I wanted someone to goose God and make him help *all* those who suffer. I *was* healing. My wrists weren't Dachau thin. I levitated up and stumbled to the mirror on the wall near the television. There I was, chubby, unshaven, minus one gangrenous gall bladder.

Life went on so I strapped on the tube: some yahoo in Waco didn't want visitors. He would not answer his door to stormtroopers until God said OK. He owned weapons. Automatic weapons. He was middle-aged and knew how to use them. He wanted America to go away and leave him the hell alone but it wouldn't the feds said, it couldn't the feds said. I clicked off the tube and heat faded away. My fevers had gone and found a new host.

XI

Two years later I wondered what had become of the one who tried to decipher the greatest work of fiction without the aid of *Cliffs Notes?* Pray tell, had he squealed off into the sunset in that classic Chevy Camaro the FBI scoffed at over the national airwaves and then rode tanks over? Did he blaze off to crack the envelope of visionary carburetion or was he merely hiding out and gathering strength, waiting for the final, apocalyptic vision of Jehovah Himself, inside his own screaming, heaven-stroked, and flame-belching Camaro, returned to earth to kick ass and later take names?

III

CORRAL OF FLAME HORSES

Some of What We Have Forgotten

*"You are fools, you die like rabbits when the hungry wolves
hunt them in the hard moon."—Chief Shakopee*

There is so much we have forgotten.
There is so much we have forgotten.
Sometimes you want to scream . . .
Dream of possibilities,
shake that crystal orb and let snowflakes
lighten the darkness of your dying
heart within.

Sometimes you want to scream . . .
Ream the possibilities
and run buck naked
into a snowbank and explode
a blinding blizzard upon the world
by using nothing more
than your natural gas.

There is so much we have forgotten.
So damn much that I have forgotten.

Listen!
The cawing of crows
is the first sign of spring.
It is a sign of rain when horses
chase and kick each other.
When the owl calls your name
there is no cure for that.

In the meantime, remember this:
Take one teaspoon of sugar
and one drop of kerosene for a bad cough.
For earache, blow smoke into the ear.
For diarrhea, cook rice and drink the juice.
Or, drink a thin paste of flour and water.
Boils: pat raw bacon rind over them.
For warts, apply castor oil.
For ghosts, burn sweet grass.
Snake bite: slice a chicken through the breast.
Lay it over bite to draw out poison.
Chicken pox, measles: bathe in soda water.
Allergy: big leaves of sage will dry rash.
Listen, you can only pray for yourself
by praying for others.
This is important above all else.
There is so much we have forgotten.
Daisy: crushed leaves on bruise will relieve pain.
For a cut with infection: chew tobacco
and spit on the open wound.
Or, make a bread and milk poultice.
Cuts and tears: use turpentine.
Eczema: mix fat and rose petals.
Poison Ivy: the juice in the leaf
and stem of the Jewill weed.
Always share your food with others.
Never refuse when food is offered.
Whooping cough: use mares' milk.
For coughs: Fry onions, wrap in flannel,
put on chest. Or, boil the bark

from the chokecherry tree and drink it.
The sap from the pine tree
makes a good gum.
The roots of cattails can be eaten
like potatoes or dried for bread.
The root of the soap weed (yucca)
is used for soap and shampoo.
Sunflower seeds can be ground into flour.
Dandelion stems can be chewed like gum.
Be strong for your woman;
not strong against her.
Brothers, be strong for your woman;
not strong against her.
There is so much we have forgotten.
Bulbs of the wild violet give
a good flavoring to soup.
Chew the root of the purple coneflower
for toothache, for bellyache,
to stop perspiration, and quench thirst.
Boil daisy fleabane
for sore mouths of children.
Buffalo berries may be stored
up to five years without spoiling.
Buzzard oil is used for eye treatment.
The root of the gum weed
is boiled for liver problems.
Heavy drinking people
poison their children.
In blindness there is always an echo.
Heavy drinking people

poison their children.
In blindness sometimes there is a third echo.
Heavy drinking people
poison their children.
Jack-in-the-Pulpit plant is good
for sore eyes.
Wild rose is brewed for eyewash.
If you see a ghost
that is what causes a stroke.
Sometimes a blind man is lucky.
Rosewater tea is good for sleep,
rest, and skin disorders.
Boil wild phlox
for laxative.

Listen.
The cawing of crows
is the first sign of spring.
It is a sign of rain when horses
chase and kick each other.

WANBLI GLESKA WIN

Eagle woman:
Wanbli Gleska Win.
Distant and unseen
in the air the piercing
whistle of an eagle taunts.

It's been six months
since you shut the door
of your flesh to me and I miss
your calm brown strength,
your high-cholesterol cooking,
the fragrant down beneath your wings
and that snake-eating beak
between your Sioux thighs.

THE FINE PRINTING ON THE LABEL OF A BOTTLE OF NONALCOHOL BEER

Then through an opening in the sky we were shown all the countries of the earth, and the camping grounds of our fathers since the beginning. All was there—the tipis, the ghosts of our fathers, and great herds of buffalo, and a country that smiled because it was rich and the white man was not there.
—Mato Anahtaka

The Redskins are winning
and I'm on the couch waiting for
the second half of their grunt-tussle
against the Chiefs to begin.
By ancient Indian habit,
I dash to the fridge for more suds.
For five years running now,
it's been this sad, nonalcohol beer
for me and my liver.
As usual, I read the health warning
before I drink the ersatz brew.
On the bottle's label, it says:

My brother, you are pouring
this illusion down your throat
because you are an alcoholic child
of alcoholic parents and they
were the alcoholic children
of your alcoholic grandparents.
My brother, oh, my brother
before your grandparents,
your great-grandparents

lived without firewater,
without the ghost of electricity,
without the white man's God
in bow and arrow old-time days.
Days of obsidian. Days of grace.
Days of buckskin. Days of grace.
Days of the war lance and the buffalo.
Days before your people learned
how to hotwire
the Great Spirit
with chemical prayers.

Cocaine Obit

The high plains sun was seduced
into January thaw and after two hours
of chopping ice on his driveway,
Jake Red Horse fell asleep on his couch
only to be awakened by furious ghosts
punching his frantic Sioux heart.
These were not comic-book friendly ghosts.
They were malevolent spirits who exploded
all the light bulbs in his house
and then spritzed through dark air
slicing at his eyes with straight razors.
He tried fighting back, but he knew
that he was up shit creek.
These spirits were programmed to kill.
Pleas to God could not stop the unholy terror.
He thought his heart would explode
before they cut out his eyeballs
and okay, you guessed it, it did.

ON THE PULSE OF MOURNING

God damn sweat-dreaming, psychedelic . . .
It was '69 and I was down scoring
keys in the Hotel Française
in Guadalajara until
a thousand whitefaced cows woke
me to this staid, prairie midlife.

Maybe tonight, it ain't my night.
2:30 A.M. and invisible seas
come crashing, filling my ears
with the moans of the dying
so I get up from my high plains
couch and call the owner
of the feed lot to wake him
secondhand to the death songs
of his sloe-eyed, night-screaming
cattle bound to be ground
into vein-clogging vengeance
and then I turn on the tube
and CNN is replaying the inaugural
doggerel of Maya Angelou.
Maybe tonight, it ain't my night.
Maybe tonight belongs to no one.
Maybe tonight history moves so fast
that no one on earth can grasp it except
the dream ghost of Violetta Vasquez
in my bed in that hotel room

almost twenty-five years ago.
Her brown chamois skin.
Her desperate *indio* eyes.
Her sparsely haired vise.
Her repetition of every inane
American phrase I uttered.
"Right on, take me San Francisco,"
she said over and over.
"Right on," I said, but never did.

And now, right now, despite
the thousand bellowing cows down the road,
Violetta raises her head up from these lines
and moistens my middle-aged cock
with her tears.

SONNY'S PURPLE HEART

But it's too late to say you're sorry.— *The Zombies*

I

Man, if you're dead, why are you leading
me to drink after five sober years?
Sonny, can I get a witness?
I had a Snow White vision of the prodigal
son returning to America
that day of my final hangover.
I tried to clear the mixture
of cobwebs and shooting stars
from my brain with spit-warm
Budweiser, but the hair of the dog
just was not doing the trick.
I ended up pummeling myself
seven times that day and named each egg
white load for a Disney dwarf.
The first was Dopey.
The final was Sleepy, I think, or Droopy.

II

Last year you scrawled a letter to me
about your first and final visit
to the Vietnam Memorial and how your eyes
reflected off the shiny black stone
and shot back into your brain like guidons
unfurling the stench of cordite and the boy screams
of men whose souls evaporated
into morning mists over blue-green jungles.

You had to be there, you said.
That's where you caught the cancer, you said.

III

Sonny. Tonight I had a dream of Mom's death
twenty years too late and now my eyes
will not close like I imagine the lid
on her cheap casket did.
I was not there when she died.
Home on leave from Basic Training,
you stood in for me
because I was running scared
through the drugged-out alleys of America,
hiding from those Asian shadows
that would finally ace you and now, now
in the dark victory of your Agent Orange cancer,
it gives me not one ounce of ease
to say fuck Nixon and Kissinger,
fuck all the generals and all
the armies of God and fuck me,
twenty years
too late.

IV

History is history and thank God for that.
When we were wise-ass American boys
in our fifth grade geography class,
we tittered over the prurient-sounding
waves of Lake Titticaca . . . *Titti . . . ca-ca*
and we never even had the slightest

clue that Che was camping out
en las montañas de Bolivia . . .
We never knew American chemists would
kill you slicker than slant-eyed bullets.

V

Damn Sonny. Five sober years done squeaked
by like a silent fart and I'm on autopilot,
sitting in a bar hoisting suds with ghosts,
yours and my slowly evolving own.
When we were seventeen with fake I.D.'s,
we got into the Bucket of Blood
in Virginia City and slurped sloe gin fizzes
while the innocent jukebox blared
"She's Not There" by the Zombies.
Later that drunken night you puked purple
splotches onto my new, white Levis
and a short, few years into your future
this lost nation would award
you two purple hearts,
one of which your mother pressed
into my hand that bright day
we filed you under
dry desert dirt.

JACK KEROUAC IN COMPUTER HELL

Reborn unto a gray crackling world
he stood and stretched and said,
"I am no longer an agoraphobic
lizard and my cock will now slice."
He surveyed the scene as best he could.
It was a world of sparkling gray with
no men, no trees, no crackhouses
and no clouds as far as he could see.
There was no up and down, but he
sensed an outside, another dimension.
He imagined a mirror before him and
then he fashioned a thought-axe.
He stared at the creature in the mirror.
It was not swollen and futile as he
had been on his morning of death.
He was handsome and halfback firm.
His dark eyes brooded pussy poems,
to have and to be rolled together.
It was time to crack the eggshell.
He swung the axe into the mirror
and crawled through into technicolor.
He was alive again in a living world.
There were things to do, bottles to drain,
critics to tie up and castrate.

First he would need some wheels.
A gray '89 Thunderbird would do.

Thunderbird because of the name.
Gray because, well, in a world of black
and white, it was equally hated by all.
White cars were cool in summer, and
reflected the melting heat, but when winter
strolled in they turned to cubes of ice.
Black cars ate ice and snow in December,
but in July they bubbled like tar pits.
Gray would trick the gods.
It would mirror away the summer sun.
Ice would ignore it in winter, avoiding
incest, thinking it part of the family.

The T-Bird was a hot knife, slicing
the black butter road of return.
He sat naked behind the wheel and turned
on the radio. Rap singers babbled inanely.
He giggled and pushed the channel selector.
A chorus of moping hillbillies yodeled
a saga of GED love strife.
This was better than Hell, this living.
He snapped his fingers and drove on,
knowing that someday he could
grow up to be president.
First, he'd need college again.
No Ivy League crap this time.
But damn. He heard a siren wailing.
A state trooper was in his rearview mirror.
Huh? He hadn't imagined this.
This was real, fear-sweat visceral.

Yeah, he'd imagine the cop to be female,
maybe Marilyn Monroe in sequined green gown.
Yeah . . . but Christ, it wasn't her at all.
It was a crew-cut, dark-glassed ape.
An ape with a huge blue pistol.
This was very disappointing. Very.
The trooper asked for his license.
He didn't have one. Didn't have a wallet
and didn't have a hand. His groin was evaporating.
He moaned for a moment, then all was silent.
He surveyed the scene as best he could.
It was a world of sparkling gray with
no men, no trees, no crackhouses
and no clouds as far as he could see.
There was no up and down, but he
sensed an outside, another dimension,
but even that was a lie.
He tried to reimagine the mirror
but nothing came.
He snapped his skeletal fingers
and sad dust fell, so he tried to quit thinking
but he couldn't, just fucking couldn't.

ELECTRIC GENOCIDE RAP

The vagabond who's rapping on your door
is standing in the clothes that you once wore.
—Bob Dylan

I

No sense crying. America is dying.
We huddle in the most violent
nation in the history of human
constipation.

Television controls our groins, our
minds. Our dreams are not our
own, electricity blinds. Nightmares
no longer derive from the blood
and we lamely ponder if that's bad
or good.

II

No sense in crying. America is
dying. At the corner of Grant and
Columbus, the excavation of the
street by sewer workers seeking
stagnation unearthed an ambushed
Marine patrol. One of the leather-
fleshed corpses, hand still in control,
grasped a brass Zippo lighter tar-
nished green though *Ira
Hayes—Semper Fi* could still
be seen.

I stared at the lighter, thinking that some street person would get past the stinking flesh and snatch it up to sell. And one bum grabbed this sure ticket to hell. From an alley, Indian jarheads in fatigues appeared. A sergeant grabbed the wino by his puke-flecked beard and put a .45-caliber slug into his head for the heinous crime of robbing the dead.

III

No sense in crying. America is dying. Our dreams are no longer our own. Oh, if only in linear progression I'd grown up and there were unbroken lines from my past to now so I could know exactly where to cast to catch that buried jar of aggies and puries I planted then, hoping that my childhood furies would abate and in some future incarnation I'd return and claim them, sure of my destination and able to decipher the scrawls of gladness I blurbed to women whose thighs salved my sadness.

IV

No reason for crying. America is
dying. In a trunk in my sister's attic
are stored unfathomed fractions,
cross-referenced forward and
unsolved to this day, this April
morning when my toilet backs up
without any warning and I yearn for
the outhouse I used till my teens
and the ultimate pleasure after a
supper of beans to sit and target
practice out the door with my .22
and my pants to the floor.

I shot tin cans (blue troopers on
steeds) and invisible ancestors
cheered my good deeds. Nothing in
my life has ever quite matched it.
That sharpness of gunpowder and
human shit mingling in that crisp
Indian air. The perfume of hope
crusted over with small scabs of
despair.

But now, no sense in crying.
America, Darling . . . you're finally
dying.

CORRAL OF FLAME HORSES

I

That night in a high plains saloon
in Lawrence, Kansas when Crazy Horse
encountered the angry skinhead
he decided there was no need
to proceed procedurally . . .

Tasunke Witko wore red braid winds
and the caucasian chrome dome
lurched stinking drunk
against the bar and roared
"I can kick any Indian's butt."

Crazy Horse talked to me later
and said he wished
he had thrown a beer in the dude's face
or at least kicked him in the *cohones*
and shoved him down
on the ground, but he didn't.
He just grabbed his old lady
and headed out the door,
got in his car, pounded the steering wheel
and months later lamely joked to me,
said, "How could you scalp a bald man?"
Well, I had no answer. He hadn't told me
about pounding his steering wheel.

His wife had, so I had her.
Only the strong chiefs survive.

II

THESIS STATEMENT: The romantic American West, that purple-saged cowboy stage where upright and rugged individualists of European descent carved out their God-given empires with six-guns blazing never existed. All the Hollywood illusion, from Tom Mix to John Wayne to Robert Redford, is simply bullshit, political and mercantile at its core, as has been the bulk of serious literature devoted to the West. Thus, the question arises: what was and is the West? What is the essence of that land and spirit which constitutes the backbone of the American identity? *Beans*. Kidney, pinto, or Anasazi beans. *Beans* are the essence of the American west. Come here dear fathers and mothers of skinheads and take a deep Dachau whiff.

III

SECOND ATTEMPT: THESIS STATEMENT.
In his extended and excellent reading of the Lawrence situation, Crazy Horse immediately grasped that the "white West is not the Indian West" and here we have a theme which never runs through any of his wife's days with me. In a nutshell and beyond any conversation of quaint manifest destiny, primitivism, or cultural colonialism, for the Indian the West was simply home and not

the *new frontier,* not the European model for a new hope. This perception is not new but is essential to understanding the West as depicted in much of American literature: in the primitivist and colonial eye, the European is complex, sophisticated, civilized; the native is the obverse, childlike, innocent, natural. This is the mechanism of control and children must be controlled, educated. It is why General Philip Sheridan could say in 1873 of the buffalo hunters, ". . . for the sake of lasting peace, let them kill, skin, and sell, until the buffalos are exterminated. Then your prairie can be covered with the speckled cattle, and the festive cowboy, who follows the hunter as the second forerunner of an advanced civilization."

IV

Well, Lord, Lord, Lord Christ,
let's close out this account.
Today I heard a high plains descendant
of Sheridan shrug his red neck
and tell his sad joke about
"Indians being the end-product
of runaway slaves having had sex
with the buffaloes . . . "
I know many Indians
who would be offended by that joke.
Myself, I'd be proud
if my father was a black

man and my mother was a buffalo.
I'd dance in my darkness and paw
the ground until my hooves reached
the corrals of the flame horses
at the molten core of the earth.
I'd round them up
and free them and we'd gallop
together across the plains of eternity
giggling, farting, and flesh-baking
anyone who stood in our path.

for Michael Harper

For My Brothers and Sisters

Indians ain't got no sense.
Indians.
Indians ain't got no new cars.
Indians.
Indians ain't owning computers.
Indians.
Indians is Indians.